BEYOND THE SCARS & CRIPPLES:

A CELEBRATION FOR ALL SEASONS

Poetry, Drawings, Songs & Essays

By AL BECK

*For Ruth Ann
a gift from
your DAD
WARM WISHES
Al Beck*

With courage and prayer
on History's most
impossible occasion,

We must prepare to be
touched by the language
of gentle persuasion

LORIEN HOUSE
P.O. Box 1112, BLACK MOUNTAIN NC 28711

copyright © 2005

by AL Beck

First Edition   July 2005

ISBN 0-934852-73-1

Library Of Congress Control Number
2005928998

Art and text are by AL Beck

Book Cover and other photographs
have been enhanced by computer
by Carmen Federowich

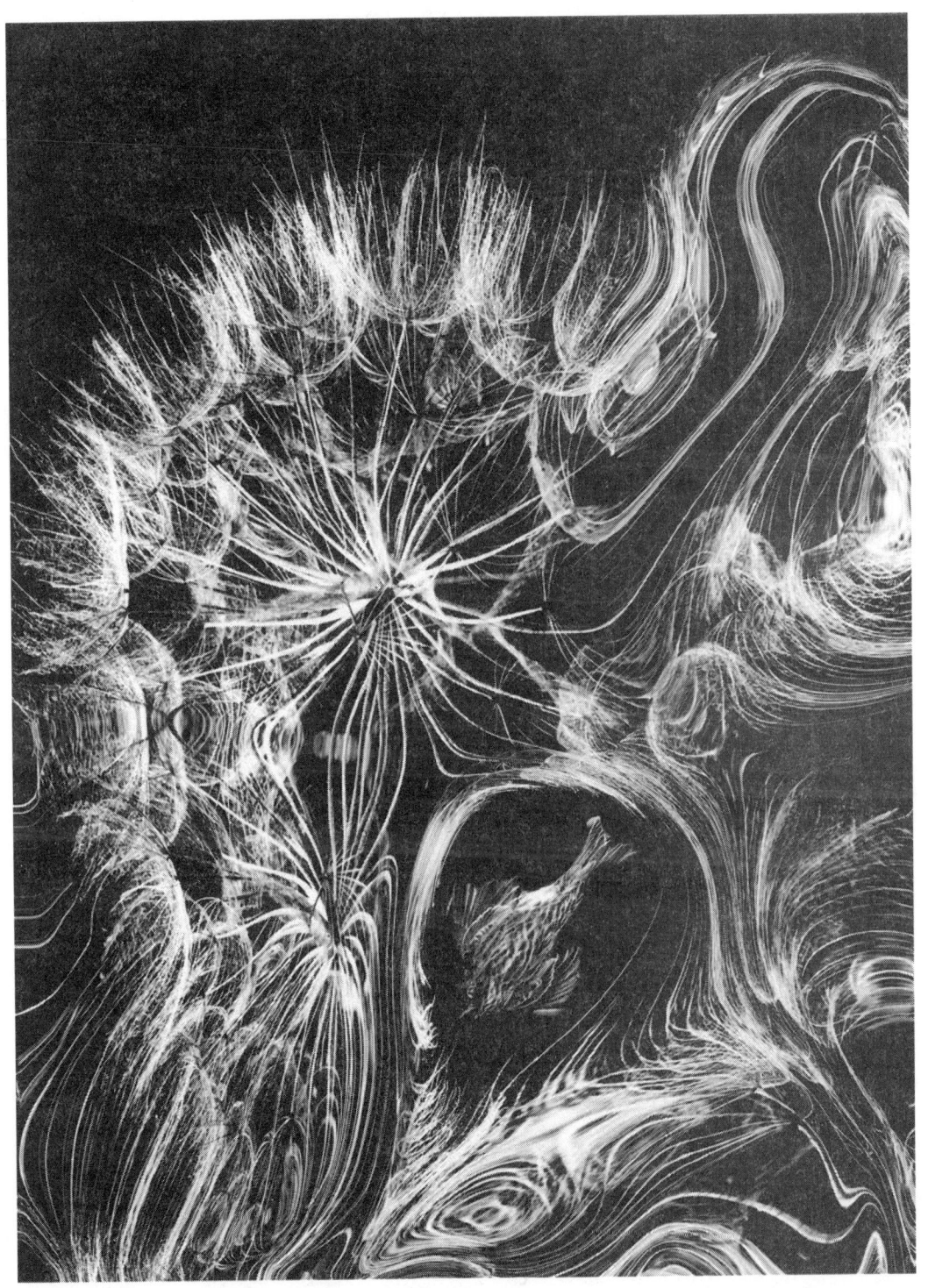

STARRY FLIGHT

Introduction

On occasion the bold invasion of common sense by an imaginative offense, I'm told, is worth its weight in mental gold.

What a wellspring of experience will do for a person who cannot ignore the past speaks volumes (pun intended) to this papers' passion. A body of knowledge hardly competes with the ancient struggles afflicting my physical body at this time of life. However, the book's title is more a message from the mind which has its own rumination resources in which to verbally dip and share a sullen sip.

The title of my eleventh book is only coincidentally related to the term 'stars and stripes' as it refers to our nation's flag. Although anyone must come to terms with the struggles our country has had over its 200 year-plus history as it might also apply to the book title. The fact remains that I can only speak to my own short history on this earth and for those who shared their ignominious moments and indomitable spirit with me.

My words are the colors of a verbal palette. I am convinced no one person can be a writer/artist without experimenting with their value, hue and intensity.

In the years of my upbringing, the world of other sensate experiences (music, texture, taste) overshadowed the intellectual/analytical facet of the human condition. (How I got through formal education is beyond comprehension). This dreamer/imaginationist played with the sensate until logic became a disease. There - I've said it - and I think I mean it.

To make one's writing undergo the demanding eye of a traditional critic is only acceptable up to a point because I feel the urge to maintain this personal edge.

Foreword

We need to develop a frame of reference for challenging those ideologies which would lock us into closed systems of thought and action and thereby strip us of the freedom of imagination to envision a new world. The effect of myopic thinking has negatively influenced society in many respects; including virulent international violence, heretical turmoil in politics, scars produced by educational oligarchy, and gripes from indiscriminate fanatics.

Permit me to share with you some thoughts on the *Commando Chemistry* corrupted by opportunistic cultural spin. When I was a kid, mythological heroes included the Bible's young David and radio's Lone Ranger. Too many supposed reasonable adults today have carried hyperbole and literary illusion into their lives as Reality – presently supported by entertainment's technologic advancement (perhaps an unsolicited device?).

Our country's leaders as well as many citizens are confusing the world of Superman and Lone Ranger exploits (aided by their "faithful companions") with reality's limitations. Many are completely convinced via well-ensconced self-delusion that America's leaders have some sort of super-natural power to erase Evil from the face of the earth. Avaricious authority figures as well as terrorists are indeed poisons on the human scene. Until we find an appropriate antidote, we must be cautious not to destroy all humanity in the process.

Dedication

It is with a sense of optimism, blessed as I have been with good friends and wise mentors, that I choose to dedicate this book to whatever idiosyncratic Power put me on this planet. Beyond the scars and gripes I may have had over a lifetime, my limitations have been a challenge through which to express feelings with poem, drawing, song and story.

INTERPOSITIVE PHASE

Carmen Federowich is the guest artist who has developed a special photographic imaging technique with a combination of computer manipulated imagery and oil paint. In her words: "After either scanning film images or downloading from my digital camera, I work with them in Photoshop where I make extensive alterations – or not. I then print out black and white interpositives which I use to produce negative images on watercolor paper with gum bichromate. I then apply oil paint to bring up a positive image. The images here are reproductions of several interpositives which stand up well in their own right, I feel."

APPRECIATION

The list begins to grow. Of course my publisher David Wilson heads the team of those who have helped to bring this book into print. Richard Holmes continues his magic with words and phrases as he makes the kind of suggestions which give a polish to sometimes iconoclastic thoughts I invent. Carmen Federowich did more this time than the cover design. A creative touch with photographic imagery is her blessed contribution to my latest work. Encouraged by William Fox, President of Culver-Stockton College, I improved several essays and an editorial. Inspired by author and computer journalist Remy Benoit, I included some of her thoughts in my book as well. And finally, permit me to mention my three grandchildren: Christopher, Samuel and Keimi who have inspired me to peek beyond the scars and gripes of present day struggles into a future of multiple positive possibilities.

TABLE OF CONTENTS

Savant-speak is
sometimes babble-bleak in the
land of Nouveau-bourgeois.

NYCHTHEMERAL* NATURE NURTURED

***From the Greek - a rare adjective
meaning that which occurs by a variation
as extreme as night and day**

Spring comes tripping into
The woods like angina to my body.

I feel a surge of winter's strain
To remain with us. So shoddy.

Maybe the pain I experience is
An empathy for first flowers

10

Which, occasionally, must tolerate
A late snow or frost. What's lost,

I celebrate in April's arrival
Despite the cost. It is my mind

Melting layers of psychic ice
And warm thoughts for refreshing

New birth which precludes any
Discomfort. And that's nice.

Spring rain and trees' leaves;
cheer nature's mellow duet
performance: Bravo!

11

FLORA – ESSENCE

I live in deep woods with
feet on the ground,
an eye on the sky and
dreams to be found

in leaf beds for Fall,
sweet bird songs in Spring
and oak trees grown tall;
Summer's harvest will bring

baskets of peppers, greens, squash,
ripe tomatoes, rich grain. Blame
persistent prestidigitation (Gosh!)
of sun's heat, plus some rain.

13

Soil's the best teacher
- of that there's no doubt -
each seed's a mental creature
patiently poised for fresh sprout.

I never rake leaves nor
ever shovel cold snow.
Nature rolls up its sleeves making
mulch in which plants grow.

My related responsibility
(if you want to call it that)
is to develop an agility
to eat it all without getting fat.

Missouri's Aprils
are mystery; suddenly
frost is history.

I'm driving through woods;
deer leaps into the car's path –
misses instant wrath.

May ends in soaking
downpour; garden's grateful for
its timely torrent.

water bird's warble
grows to whirl beyond it's own
sphere; chaos theory

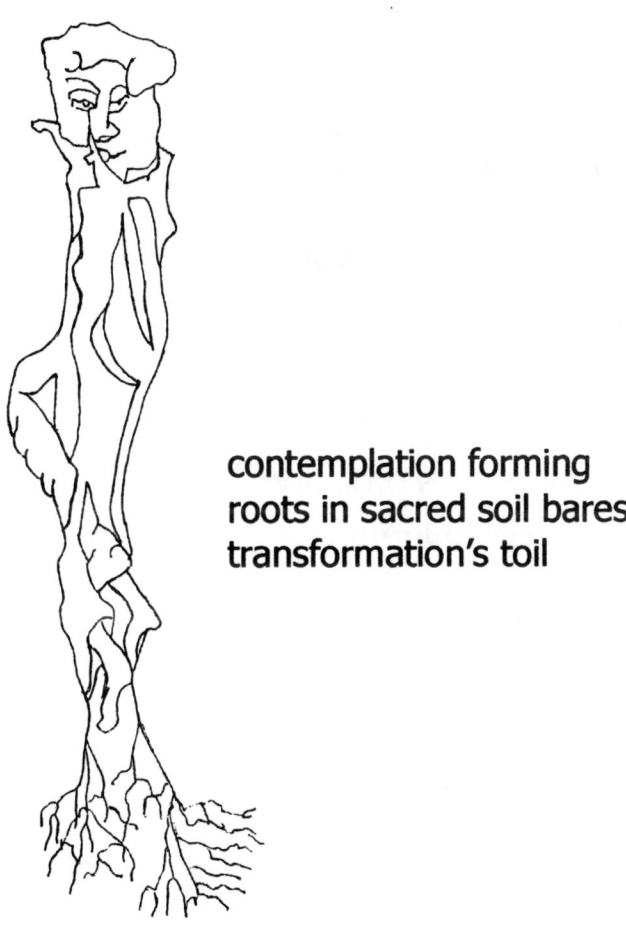

contemplation forming
roots in sacred soil bares
transformation's toil

Distant growl in a
dark sky. The air sweats like a
wrestler; storm's coming.

Season's socket for
Spring planting quickly slinks
Into summer's pocket.

As predawn thunder
Grumbles nervously joined by
Rain's active applause,

Lightning replaces
Rising sun's ordinary
Exercising jaws.

It is, finally, Nature's goal
To take control.

uninterrupted
crickets ignore prediction
of night's thunderstorm.

Summer temporarily
abandoned its plan
to wallow in
humid heat.
Instead, tonight
slipped on a cool jacket
and we all
did a dance
to a mental,
gentle beat.

summer's sun nests in
the west; winds blow while sea's waves
show their final glow

some ideas are
simply bound to fail: don't try
saddle on a snail

Not yet sunrise
On Dauphin Island

Sand, sea and sky
Blend soft hues
Of common darkness
(interrupted above by
pinpointed pearls of light)

While below, a sea 'n beach
Duet sings its special song.

Now water, wind and sandy beach
Each declare rare pledges
To share their momentary
Organic edges —

Leaving only fragile,
Disappearing white necklaces
Of foam on a surface
Of its earthly home.

You see, they're on a temporary spree
And so, my friends, are we.

morning wind: cool fingers
tickle ocean waves - giggle
when they ripple

FLIGHT DELIGHT

I'm sitting by the ocean
with a notion that
each grain of sand speaks
silently for aspects of eternity.
Sun, sky, shoreline, water
with a single purpose seeks
universal fraternity.

Oh the shapes of sea-worn wood
carved with care (as only God could).
And such stories He might tell
of surf-sliced footprints
or soul-stirring's solitary shell.

I note with sadness
a similarity in the human race
where Time's high tide
has, on occasion, swept aside
precious muted memories
and left a trace
of flotsam's face.

stars and surf's sounds blend
my senses; night's enchantment
blurs mental fences

Darkness – a wet tongue
hovering over our island.
It licks the air
covering sea, surf, sand and,
discovering its season of
mystic energy,
invisibly penetrates
every element of reason.

sea water ripples
in foamy chords; moving fingers
massage the shores

Crabapple tree
wet with rain
from an afternoon's
dark sky bleeder.

Sleepy white cat
raises his head
notes humming bird
dodging drops

as it zips to its
sheltered feeder.
Showers do clean
the air but more

than sanitizing;
they perform a gentle
tapping sound
on leaf and ground

which some
might consider
wondrously
mesmerizing.

in our woods a sound
absurd; since squirrels don't squeal,
must've heard a strange bird.

August's gypsy
breezes drift from tree to tree;
leaves silently rattle.

Autumn's tenacious
tongue licks away at shag bark
hickory leaf's life.

on a cool September
morning, I feel better
wearing a sweater.

On September's stage,
full moon lights up a quiet
colorful leaf choir

behold midnight
crickets' chorus; despite our
sleepless pique, ignore us.

in the woods flooded
by a full moon, what bliss is
this to take a piss.

trunk bones and branches
twitch in November's wind;
dead leaves – winter's chagrin.

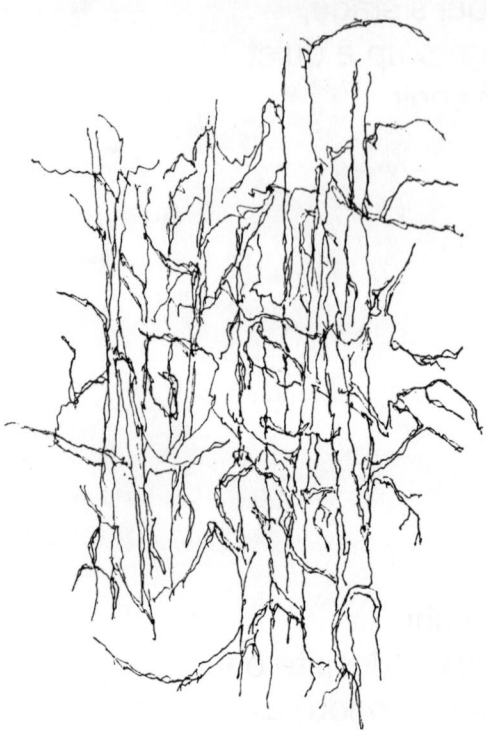

Late fall, just before
November snarls at us,
A thermometer reads
Sweet sixty-two;
Brown leaves quietly
Carpet the ground.
Trees having turned to
Duller line and shadow,
Contrast willingly with
Cardinal's stark color.
It's a season when Nature's
Harvest will satisfy; as
Reluctantly Reality
Heaves a heavy sigh.

emissions may be
my bag; but, I confess,
global warming's a drag

sounds of a distant
train's whistle shiver in
November's morning air

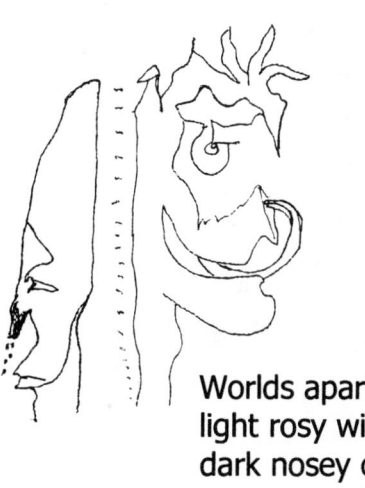

Worlds apart:
light rosy witticism –
dark nosey criticism.

Man observes
Trees' leaves wither

Trees sense arrival
Of another winter

Winter watches an approaching
fragile season in man

broken branches still
cling to tree; won't bear leaves this
spring – that's plain to see.

Late February -
a soft northwest wind shivers;
pond's surface quivers.

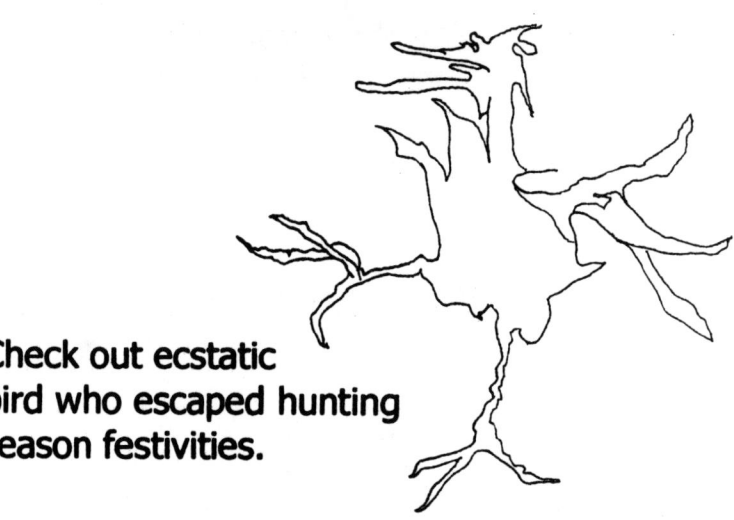

Check out ecstatic
bird who escaped hunting
season festivities.

Squirrel cuddles on
branch next to tree trunk; huddles
against heartless winter.

winter watching wrens
at a feeder; almost nothing
could be sweeter.

Winter's raw claw is
Replaced by Spring's quiet paw
As I stand in awe.

germination:
prepare for spring planting; be
alert to seeds' frail tails.

Is it the sun
or heavenly glue
which keeps us in our orbit?

It's probably
the glue because
there's apparently

no galactic source
available
to absorb it.

wasp works wings in windless
air; exhausting as spring
planting – I was there.

Hunters may wild
turkeys flush but fresh blood's in
new redbud blossoms' blush.

though in early spring
cool lingers, fresh green's on
old oak's faithful fingers

unknown footprints show
on new fallen snow; a frail
temporary trail.

youngsters do like knapsacks;
older folks reverse it --
preferring sack naps.

Success in old age
is sometimes considered a
Pyrrhic victory.

How not to forget
when our age is a threat?
Paste a note on your nose.

REASONING WITH SEASONING

It is one a.m. I stumble to
Where one sits at a keyboard and
Fumble with my wits in starts and fits.

Determined I'll write an e-mail
To my now-grown-up son.
Somewhat concerned I might fail,

Mind avoids a chance to preach.
Instead I'll struggle to reach
Out into empty, even lonely space

Attempting to share a positive face
With expressions carefully tender
Of an appropriate gender.

Adult to his childhood memories flicker
As I attempt to grasp the moment but
It seems that the years are even quicker.

And in an attempt to reject the questions
Which I always hate, as I reflect:
Is it too soon, or is it too late?

Eventually I will find a way to be reasonably
Kind as I make the effort to fill this
Cyber-envelope and empty out my mind.

33

We are at History's
human ridge. Do we build
a bridge or fall off?

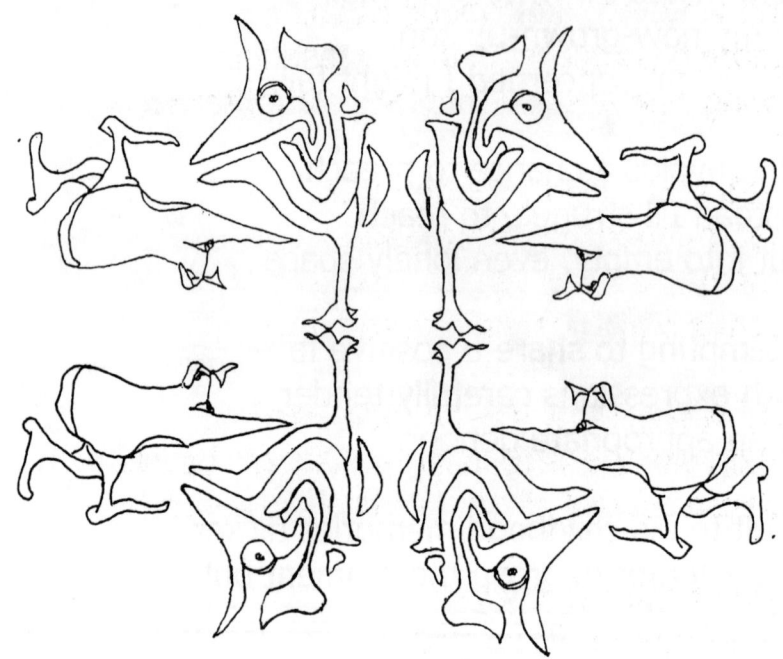

confrontation from
any angle is an
enigmatic tangle

how long can a
culture remain before it
circles history's drain?

CLASSROOM CHIMERA

Intelligence drips from Education's jaws
as this classroom Chimera with its
No-child-left-behind claws tears at the
framework of the learning experience.

And watered in a robotic ritual,
ignoring compassion in any fashion,
young humans are mentally slaughtered.

Life's tools must include more
than memorized information.
Empathy as well as Accountability
is critical to successful maturation.

And what about Inspiration's role?
When will these drooling pedagogic beasts
release control of the child's psyche-rights

long enough to permit
some right brain insights?

poem by Al Beck (c 2005)

Independent thinkers
trapped in neo-con's social
cage; how they rage!

Spirit Revisited

It was on my uncle's farm
In a world of tall corn stalks
It seemed it would do no harm
If I raced through them down the hill
Gathering momentum at will
Unaware of future's symbolic alarm

At merely four years of age
Unaffected by youthful energy,
How would it help this human rabbit engage
And thereby possibly have known
The implications these seeds had sown
As they impacted upon an upcoming page?

Isolated from political confusion
With canoe rides, campfires, walks in the park
Around life in-eighty-seconds-flat's an illusion.
An artist sees without myopic conspiratorial blinders
And limited only by fragmented historical reminders,
It's fingers' touch, vision's flutter, freely uttered without intrusion

In measuring the effort for what it takes,
Of course, be assured I've had no remorse
Past pleasures wrinkled with strawberries, corn and snowflakes.
Each special season twinkled brightly Nature's morality.
Thus we've crossed Being's bridge from pretend to reality
Savoring recollected successes and regretful mistakes.

Gone, the treasure of
countless years when family
DNA disappears

Smart people know their
limitations; wise people
risk challenging them.

In a special way,
as we grow older we live
outside our bodies.

Ballad: **SEARCHIN'**

Chorus:
Oh we're looking' for answers
Searchin' everywhere.
Maybe it's the questions' fault
I'm quite confused – I swear.

1.
Time's dark soft silken shirt
Reaches beyond the nearest star;
And who really knows as a need for absurdity grows
Just where in Life we are

Ch

2.
Riding on a midnight highway,
I search the empty space ahead of the car.
Even on high beams the road ahead
Is visible just so far

Ch

3.
See, this generation's trend for
new tradition blends NOW into
all instant gratification with
growing fear of erudition.

Ch

4.
What appear to be cryptic facts
Attempting to make humanity better
Slip between cold cultural cracks.
Time to put on a sweater.

youth demands instant
superficial pleasure; age
seeks deeper treasure.

Transition

Flights of fancy speak
softer now.
Their guarded voices
understand how change
becomes more than
an idle threat.
It is said that a disturbing
silence signals new adventure
to walk quietly - giving Time
its precious space to wrestle,
even sweat, with unexpected
reflection.
Growing older can be
a gentle challenge.
Perhaps I'll sit down
and think about it.

Advice to elderly:
be stronger − hang in there
a little longer.

Every garden
dedicated to seeding
must be worth weeding

a garden without a trellis
for flourishing tomatoes
is permitting its youngsters
to grow up untied
to lattice limitations
in order to avoid normal
bickering in the struggle
for maturation.
Furthermore,
this precious fruit deserves
careful caging not to restrict
it, but to reach out for
support - giving its life
some discipline and an
opportunity to perform
indeterminately without
solipsistic ambition –
If that's what it's meant to do.

Some memories
Linger like the taste of a
Dreamy dessert's last bite.

Future's urgency's
restrained by emergence, see?
of paranoia.

Waiting in the car sipping
coffee as time passes;
check my watch
and clean my glasses
wondering where they are.
Impatience, although not
virtuous, never leaves
a visible scar

41

There are strings attached;
so shout whenever Life's music
gets you strung out.

mirror, mirror in my hand
there's an image
I can't understand.

mirror, mirror did I create
a reflection of
my strange mental state?

memories reborn:
Time-rope's loose strands rewound are
bound to make us mourn.

Psychic schemes
Of skin surface as

Physical stimulation
Spiritual enlightenment

Mental fulfillment
Creative inspiration

Feeding greedy dreams
Worshipped worlds of wonder

Emotional satisfaction
Investing in intuition

Isolated thoughts
Hope wrestling with rage.

Priority for any human's page
often alters with insight's age.

43

where mental petals
sour, we evolve to
disappointed flower.

Childhood friend writes;
Mind and time conspire. Erase years
In memory's fire.

Which are we – prone to be
afraid or merely dismayed
when a dark

energy emerges
from underneath a cloak of
external beauty ?

Anger energizes
psychic motors while it
strangles empathy.

SEED CHILD

Dialectics? If
I'm not for it, I generally
ignore it.

Lies versus Truth:
Imagination's offense or
Logical defense.

Truth's wrapped in reason;
with Fantasy, Lies are not
its only season.

Despite the well worn
shibboleth, believe no bark
is worse than a bite.

When mentally
mutilated by aggression,
call it obsession.

48

rationalization:
temporary protection
for mental wounds

Lie in bed thinking
about the day ahead and
what I'll do instead

Speculation is
like a mental quiz or a
drink that's lost its fizz

This living business is
quite a drain for sure.
Storms ravage the mental
psyche's membrane while
outside we must endure
some physical strain.

Age sheds passion swiftly
from our human uniforms.
Medical records become
more complex as a few
final pages in our earth's
registry reflects.

May it also note
this cruise ship trip
(supine-with-cool-drink-into-senility)

was certainly an illusion.
Still, I continue to ride my
life's horse at brisk trot.

Only I've got
the rein slipping
out of my finger.
So keeping my
balance requires
a mental wringer.

age reaches beyond
its misery index into
grunt gratitude.

Old habits are
almost like dead rabbits:
one's hopeless – other's hopeless.

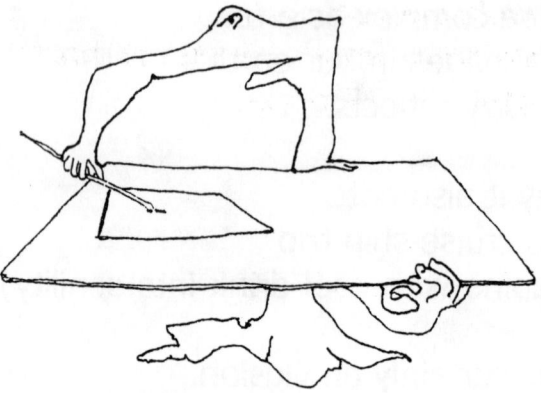

50

reptile thinking will
focus on a product rather
than the process

While growing up
balance skewed Reality
with Fantasy's escape

Hedonistic humans
hinder society's search
for Joy's future.

Should we complain
cooking in Time's kitchen without
a sink – just a drain?

debate paints the air
with gentle talks; complaints come
out as nasty squawks

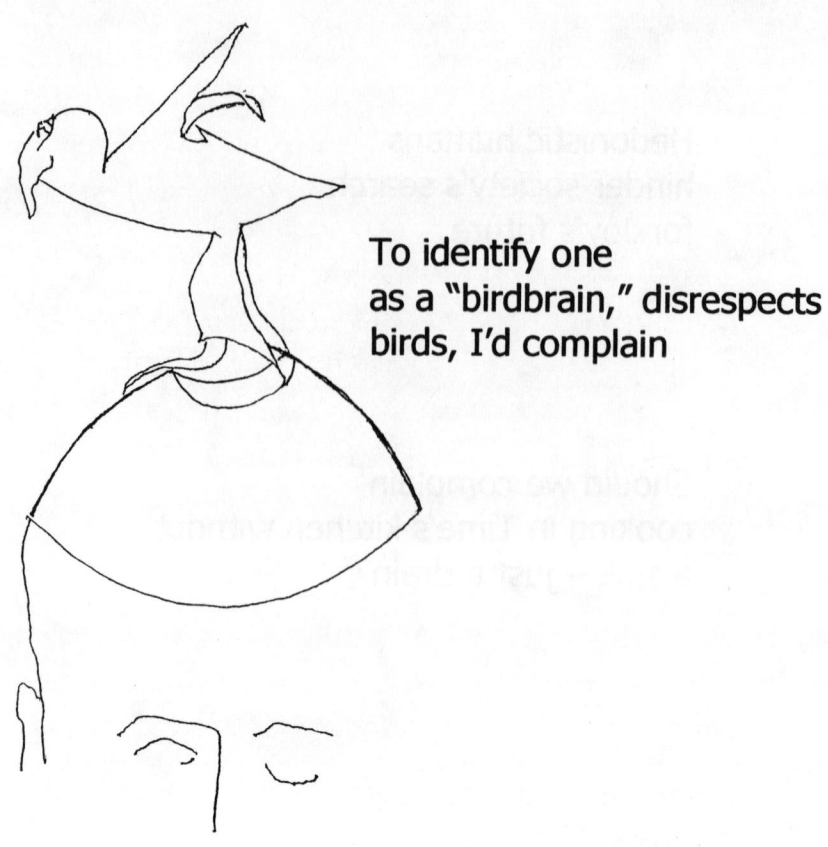

To identify one
as a "birdbrain," disrespects
birds, I'd complain

Out of touch with
Culture's shallow crock and clod;
I've grown older, thank God.

On the last day of
Its life, I wonder what
My cat will be thinking.

Very little's
considered jolly on the
good ship Melancholy.

Avoid carrying regrets
of one's past missteps
into the future like
ugly scars on the psyche.
Sorrow must be considered
a temporary wound.

53

Each moment in our existence
is a tiny piece of a much larger,
more complex panoramic continuum.
Even a single thoughtless word
spoken in haste alters not only
a communication design's immediate

and specific focus in history, but
will indirectly affect multiple
layers of all life – rearranging
every aspect of eternity. Some sad
memories may cast a temporary spell.
But, I plead, on these please don't dwell.

As I confront Death, it appears
little will change for the world
without my presence in it.

Occupying space on
this planet for a specified
time doesn't make the air
temperature fluctuate or
the rain fall more consistently
or alter the movement of stars
or even permit grass to grow
greener.

History is a human game –
Time somehow always wins.

I'll be basically the same person
in everyone's mind who knew me
"when" – who lived with me, who
worked and played with me.
But I just won't be eating cashews
and writing on paper with a pen –
as I'm doing now.

It seems Perception and Reality
have very little in common.

one never escapes
their past; even a freewheeling
iconoclast.

ASPIRE BY PUTTING DEFEAT TO THE FIRE

Potential successes
must aspire by putting
defeat to the fire

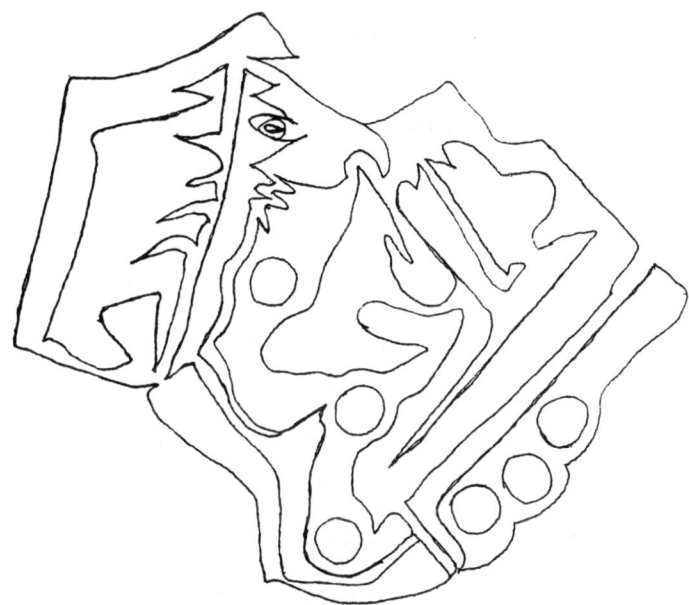

How uncommon it
is to find leaders who can
make wise decisions

and are able, without
effort, to exhale
simultaneously.

an artist sees without
myopic conspiratorial blinders
isolated from political confusion;
limited only by fragmented
historical reminders.

Dare to be alive
in a world which defies one
to be different.

Whatever you are,
wherever from, you're bound to
become – yeah, bizarre.

Insignificant
Advice more than wit: Never
Step in your own spit.

aspiration's deep
well satisfies thirst to be   57
better than we are.

expecting prize as
praise for success, desire's been
confused with aspire.

From docile to
animus, a more gentle
creature's in all of us.

Momentarily,
with collective sorrow, we
forget our conflicts.

Nasty spectators
at sports events deserve it
when Boo bird strikes back.

Cribbage

So much in living should
Prepare us to aspire.
Even a friendly game of
Cribbage helps to light a fire.

Whether shuffling cards or
A morning roll out of bed
We prepare what we hope
Helps us finally come out ahead.

Dealing to each six cards face down
Indicates you give as good as you get.
And what's a better way to say DNA
Than by putting two in a crib? (don't forget)

One's progress is measured in this game
With tiny wooden tapered pegs.
Like much in life it seems to reflect
Just when you're finally "getting your legs".

And just at the point where the game
Seems to slow down and get stuck,
It suddenly rushes forward with a good deal
Of thoughtful skill and a dollup of just plain luck.

Advice to any player: when you anticipate
Before it's over this game you have clearly lost,
Keep up your spirit and pray to avoid
A cursed double skunk at whatever the cost.

A game's more than who just won.
It's a challenge to ability.
For when all is said and done
We still celebrate compatibility.

ignoring an
occasional blunder, hear
Time's constant thunder as

life continues in
its perpetual state of
plunder and wonder.

Loyalty's river
always runs deep. It will,
never freeze over.

60

One question must be
asked: What will keep a
civilization alive?

Is it either
adversarial or
collaborative thinking

which is absolutely,
without doubt, a
necessity to survive?

Nothing bugs skanky
creatures like bearing a
burden of decency.

we may soon need more
tissues for tears over unsolved
long-term issues

find a future world
where passion and reason no
longer live apart.

Please understand, if
you ruffle my feathers, my
moon comes into view.

62

Restrain an urge to
complain when out on a limb
or protest distressed.

What often passes
for idle conversation
(sometimes defined as

"verbal play toys") can
truly translate more as mere
meaningless white noise.

when any bone
begins to moan, one must move
from vertical to prone

63

tattooed turtle moves
at his own pace; rarely fears
burn-out from a race.

A lift from worry
To just concern requires less
Mental taciturn.

Sometimes play with a
stethoscope to grope on
creativity's rope.

H.I.P. : HONORING IMAGINATION'S PALIMPSEST

64

intuition
requires more attention than
capricious invention.

when intuition
sneezes, an intellect promptly
blows its nose clean.

When a mind takes flight –
Every feather in place –
It stretches one's imagination
To the unknown limits of outer space.

No dark cloud is allowed
To interrupt the soaring.
Only gentle winds which have not sinned
May possibly be a bit too boring.

Inspiration's no roar heard from an angry dog
No growl of a bear, nor goat bleat.
But soundless cries of mental bird on the rise
As it leaves its feet – now complete.

65

Out of life's selected vessel
emerges the unexpected with
which we'll have to wrestle.

N.I.C.E. (New Intergenerational Collaborative Experiences) ™

William Safire remarked in a NY Times Op-ed column on Monday, January 24, 2005:…"And what about what the cognition crowd calls "executive transfer" in learning? Does an early grasp of the arts - music, dance, drama, drawing - affect a child's ability to apply that cognitive process to facility in math, architecture, history? New imaging techniques and much-needed longitudinal studies may provide answers rather than anecdotes and affect arts budgets in schools."

IMAGI-PLAY: ™
I-G C : Intergenerational Collaborative Learning Experiences

COLLABORATIVE THINKING BY GRANDPARENT AND GRANDCHILD

The process by which inspired thinking germinates fresh energy for enriched, longer living in the elderly while, at the same time, encouraging development of original ideas in young people.

Stories and experiences of collaboration in learning go way back in my life. I could go as far back as the English Language Classes I volunteered to teach in Taegu, Korea during my off-duty hours with the U.S. Army back in the mid '50s.

But let's bring it closer to my present senile "swinging" days. When my grandson, Christopher, was about 3 or 4 years old, I would visit him and bring a bucket of crayons and large sheets of white paper. We would sit on the floor and I would make a squiggle on the page with my "favorite" color. Then I would ask him to take his favorite color and make another part of our "collaborate" picture.

He would begin to make his own marks and imagery connecting them sometimes to mine, -- sometimes not.

I would then turn the paper and observe it from a different

direction.

Then I would do some more (not too much) additions to the "picture". Then it would be Christopher's turn. This would go on for several turns until Christopher studied the growing image and said..."Hey, gramps, it's beginning to look like a boat!" "Where?" I said...."OK, a boat it is."

"Let's keep going with our picture...but now we have an idea of what we might be making, right?"

"Right", he firmly remarked.

And we continued to alternate turns (me for shorter – less specific participation) until Christopher began to smile as the whole sea, boat and maybe a bird or two and maybe a fish and....and....And that's called adult/child collaboration in the art world.

Children can be encouraged to do this with other children. *The object is never to criticize what the other person is doing.* And give the children the opportunity to express their most creative urges.

It might be worthwhile to mention the danger and mental poison which coloring books present to young children. Once a visual "bible" is placed before a young child to color-images-within-their-lines, - the house, the horse, the dog, the tree, the whatever becomes a sacred preconception of what it *should* look like in the child's mind. Drawing it differently (imaginatively) from this preconception is unconsciously not a good thing to do in a child's subsequent experiences. The child has been "programmed" to know what the object should look like and will generally not attempt to make their own version of it.

67

Collaborative Visual Variation with Music:

Inter-sensate inspiration has natural creative opportunities when the music is without words and has passages with both high/low, fast/slow portions to it. Many classical selections would apply. The adult speaks out and says: "I hear a color in the music...hmmm, let me look through our crayons and pick out the color I hear..."

(If the child doesn't imitate the adult's actions with his/her own color choice then the adult might urge the child to pick what "color" he/she hears).

Soon after, as the music changes its character (slower/faster, higher/lower), the adult will then express a need to change his "color" and do so. "Oh, the music is changing, I hear a different color.....etc"

WRITING CREATIVE STORIES COLLABORATIVELY

I can do this with Christopher now that he is in second grade and we **write** stories in the same collaborative fashion. First I might begin with..."**Once upon a time**..." and then I stop and hand him the paper and he continues..."There was a little person"...

And I am given back the sheet: **"This person was very strange because..."**

I stop writing there to act as a stimulus for his ideas ...and hand him back the sheet: "he had yellow eyes and a green face."

He then hands me back the sheet and I write: **"One day he met a very unusual animal who..."** And Christopher takes the paper..."was like a monster with a cheetah tail and a elephant body and a bull head."

Now, I will stop the story here...I am certain you get the game we are playing. Note, please that I do not correct his spelling or his grammar or his use of incorrect articles
(a elephant)...we just keep rolling with the story.

His mother – my daughter – absolutely loved this "play" between grampa and her boy.

Now that Christopher is in third grade, we continue to do both collaborative art work as well as verbal collaborations... And it's just the beginning.

(and, **No**, I won't tell you how our story came out...sorry)
========

Note please that structure and plot are secondary considerations whereas **PROCESS IS PRIMARY**.

The adult in the team provides the continuing mental stimulus without providing a specific focus or specific direction....in other words "open-ended responses" to continue the character of the story.

It is critical that during the activity the adult partner becomes more supportive and less directive.

1. Exude a positive attitude by avoiding negative judgments
2. Develop creative directions but not solutions
3. Encourage the child with praise for visual or verbal risk

THE CHOCOLATE WITCH
by Christopher Revell and Al Beck

A very interesting thing happened today* because a witch cast a spell on me and it made me look like a *strange funny looking creature who had* a zebra head, an elephant body and crocodile legs and a dinosaur tail.

"Wow!" I cried as I looked into the mirror. "I wonder what my mother will say." Just then she opened the door and she screamed "Ahhhh!" and said to the witch "What have you done to my son?" And I tried to say, "This is your son. But I just remembered that the witch cast a spell on me. So now I only said Nahhhhh!"

His mother was angry with the mean witch and said to her son, "Why didn't you tell me earlier?"

And I said "I couldn't because I couldn't talk."

"Oh, that's right." *"But now you can" she said.*

"Do you know any magic words to get rid of that witch?" she asked. "Yes, I think I do," I said.

And I screamed loudly, because I forgot what the words were but just then remembered the words and said them *to the witch, who he knew, was afraid of anything chocolate:*

"CHOCOLATE SODA, CHOCOLATE BAR – NOW YOU CHANGE FROM WHAT YOU ARE" And guess what happened? You guessed it. She turned into a chocolate witch and then I had a chocolate sale and the witch was the chocolate and all the kids from all over the world ate her *almost all up. And the rest of the witch just melted away.*

THE END

*please note that all the words in italics were written by Al Beck and the regular word style was Christopher Revell's writing.

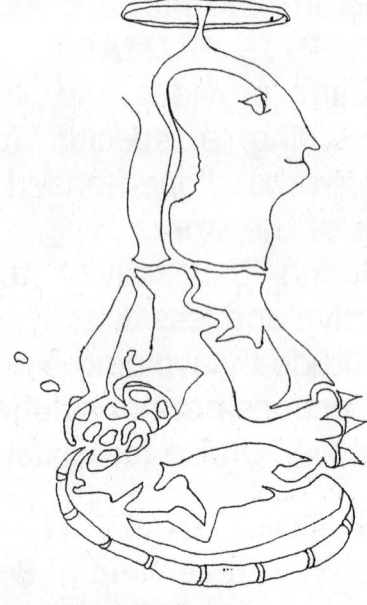

Evolutionary Icon

70

Aesthetics and
Survival Instincts are children
From different Gods.

seek a fearless flash
of insight: submit to
imagination's flight

Original
thinking leaves a conventional
mind behind stinking

DESIGN'S DEGLUTITION

Whenever my mood turns capricious
and my focus badly needs a crutch,
I try not to be too facetious when I say
"my reality's losing its touch."

Still, always in moments like this,
intuition gets actively playful.
Fresh thoughts exceed their genesis.
Music-inspired, I get carried away – full.

So I'll choose to remove well-worn shoes
and dance every tune with feet bare.
Determined to reject life's grim growling,
I'm careful what mental clothes I wear.

When sullen song's replaced by hardy howling,
I wink at graceful empty attitudes
and prepare to tolerate conservative scowling
as Reason's folly supersedes specious platitudes.

I continue to carry
mental baggage
others have chosen
to leave behind.
And while I believe
it's necessary to weave
aspects of Reality
with Imagination's "sins,"
it is said everyone wins
where Truth ends
and Conundrum begins.

WAKA form

As frog-prince holds on
to demanding young princess,
she's transformed during
a compatible moment
into a loving creature.

minds full-wired have three
colors: curiosity,
focus, energy.

Back from the edge of
extinction, he drew as his
inspiration grew.

One should have the
impulse once to recklessly
rescue rare residue.

One's spirit's shoddy
when an active mind infects
a sleepy body.

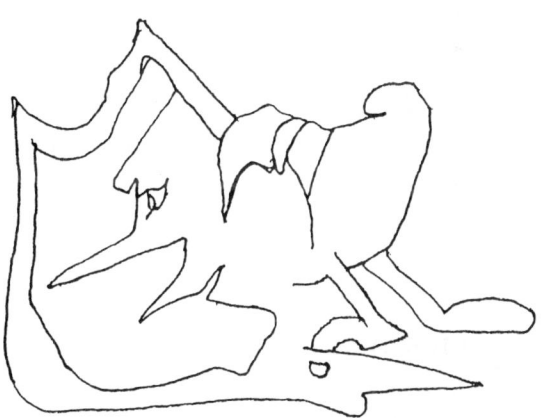

Search for Truth
in unexpected places; thus
when Curiosity embraces us,
we'll have energy to maintain
our mental youth

Creative Urge Enemies

The urge for creative expression is connected to four critical aspects of the human condition known to many as The Four Ayes (or, in some circles, as The Four "Eyes").

They are, in no particular order: Innovation, Invention, Intuition and Imagination. And in, again, no certain order are the enemies: Expectation, Perception, Preconception, Preconditioning and Assumption (or as some might transform it – Presumption).

Developing new ideas certainly demands a background of mental tools within a given discipline. However, the Enemies preclude most, if not all, opportunity to work effectively with these Ayes.

Denying Traditional thinking is a given in the world of Creative Urges.

Risk is an essential ingredient in developing innovative and inventive thought. And Failure, that poison to the analytical mind, is always an experience one can expect during the blend of Imagination and Intuition.

Thus the nature of our cultural worship for success over failure has no place in this right-brained world. Know that each of the Creative Urges' Enemies is programmed to focus on what kind of successful product can be built as efficiently as possible. Because Product is the primary rationale for any activity, the character of Process must adhere to a series of assumed steps to produce an end result.

The entire experience is a preconceived and, usually, standardized perception for an expected outcome. And thus, it is presumed to be a successful result. Mr. Logic removes his chapeau and bows most courteously.

In Imagination's Universe, very little initial energy is put into the kind of product while a great deal of energy is devoted to process.

Of course a product may well evolve from this energy. Nevertheless, if no product comes forth, much still is gained in the Creative Kingdom.

One must be committed to this special form of human growth.

PELICAN STREAM

Ancient Finger Ring

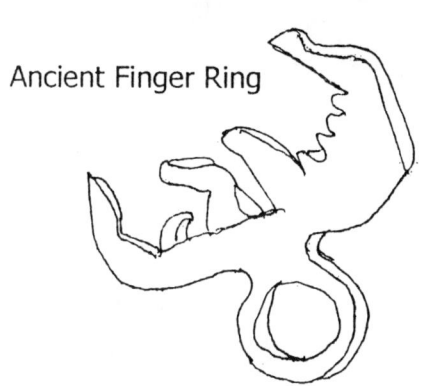

an invention
often reaches beyond its
initial intention.

Conflict's priceless
invention: revolver with
moral indigestion.

Creativity,
regretfully, may be too
thoughtful to be taught.

And, like any rare
digestive disease, cannot
easily be caught

Song: **Wabi-Sabi**

Chorus:
Wabi-Sabi, Wabi Sabi
Life reflection's a serious hobby.
Don't expect to turn 'em around;
Both good and bad are deep in our ground

---

1. Full moon does such things to my head
   Floods memory's bed and, it's like I said
   Sometimes the tears will last for years
   So concentrate on the cheers instead

Chorus

2. Never ignore a creative request
   When building mental castles, tall ones are best
   False feathered thinking ends up stinking
   Put your imagination to an outrageous test.

Chorus

3. While confusion may promote untimely regression
   A singular focus leads to obsession
   Let soft dreams drape reality's shape
   Wake to inspiration's fresh expression

Chorus

4. Originality's an enlightened state
   But with risk comes failure - part of passion's freight
   One sensitive tries to listen with the eyes
   As spiritual esthetics resonate

Chorus

Unusual birds
balance precariously
on rigid branches.

Still, they're thinking
about a world with infinite
possibilities.

An ocean, the child's
sandbox, wrinkled sheets – all speak
with unique patterns.

Some say I'm crazy –
speaking to a daisy. Hey,
Mac! They don't talk back!

Select with care what
you see; beware the bite of
an angry TV.

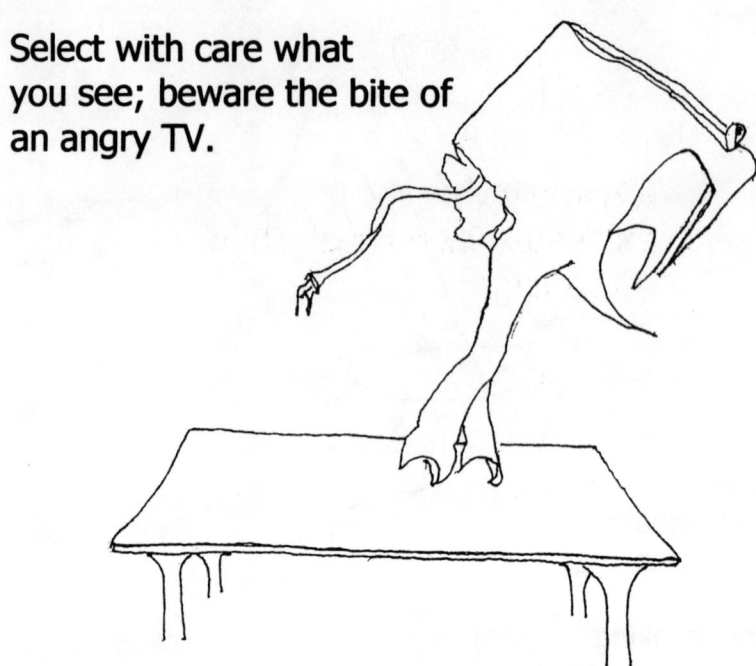

From its original
Definition, Reality's
Meaning has

Been damaged by
Television entertainment
Far beyond repair.

GRIST ONE MAY HAVE MISSED

Inhumanity's
the wage when imagination
is in a cage.

it's insulation
not isolation which expires
inspiration.

sanctimony
encourages a crash of
new idea's panache.

Status quo is planned
to emerge from our body's
bland gland. Understand?

Set in one's ways while
being opinionated
compounds ignorance.

Bureaucracy –
defined as institutional
inertia's quagmire.

Figure the cost when
Anger is our enemy:
Common sense is lost.

No doubt any
creature would start to wail when
someone's stepped on its tail.

If one lives in an
epidemic state of angst,
each day must be

Halloween

when we flutter
on fear's edge between fact
and paranoia.

NEGATIVE THINKING

Chorus one:
    Sings the doubter's song:
    "It won't work.
    Something's gotta be wrong.
    If you do it, you're a genuine jerk!"

1. Fussbudget, nitpicker
    Sour grapes inspector
    Present's a curse – future's worse,
    Disaster's prime collector
        **

    A skeptic naturally sees
    Life's turns and twists
    Some call this an attitude
    Others labeled as pessimists

Chorus One:

2. Gloomy guys prefer
    Nay to say hooray.
    Every issue has to stir
    Unique shades of grey
        **

    Don't tell me it'll work
    I'm not that blind, ya know.
    Do you take me for a jerk?
    Something wrong will always show.

Chorus two:
    Negative thinking's
    A hypochondriac's game.
    It's a beat from hoodwinking;
    But not quite the same.

3. Searching for flaws
   is delicious discontent.
   Splitting cynic's straws:
   A suspicious detriment
       **

   We're prone to note when
   Pairs don't match.
   The color may be off or
   One have a nasty scratch.

Chorus One:

4. Don't save for rainy day's reflection.
   Heck, it's always raining.
   Keep in mind that any perfection
   Usually requires retraining.
       **

   Since the future appears
   Immediately worse
   Don't you believe
   We all need a nurse?

Chorus Two:

5. Born of folks that
   could smell a lie,
   Great grandpa told Orville
   He would never, ever fly.
       **

   So raise a flag for
   The dogmatic grouch
   Whose spirit's gotta be
   In perpetual slouch.

Chorus One

seems excessively
cruel when perfection becomes
a dangerous tool.

Those who live on the
Dark edges of vanity
Rationalize their

Sanity by attempting
To define and measure
Humanity.

88

Curiosity
alters mostly minds –
Animosity? bodies.

Life is not measured
nor pleasured by years without
tears or even days

without being in
a daze; but by those moments
of light with a bite.

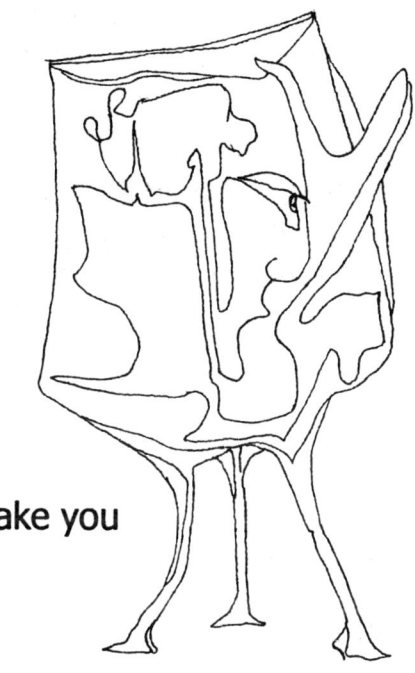

Any nasty tasting
drink might at least make you
think (or is it stink?)

Fear technology's
dark side: instantaneous
gratification.

Beware guile's treason
in any season when passion
wrestles reason.

Clone concepts
may challenge Reality's
theoretical precepts.

Turmoil is certain
to spoil any life's mixture
of water and oil.

Beyond his surface
baiting smile, be wary of
percolating guile.

Which are we – prone to be
afraid or merely dismayed
when a dark

energy emerges
from underneath a cloak of
external beauty ?

Unsolicited
advice inspires responses
rarely labeled 'nice.'

Human nature becomes
corrupted whenever
civilization's

interrupted while
thinking about divinity's
infinity

Politics is less
a slippery slope than
clinging to greased up rope.

A dark sky suggests
it's either too late or
much earlier than
when most living
things are awake.

The eyes often lack
appropriate focus under
these circumstances;
so too, many minds of limited
intelligence throughout History.

Their plodding political antics
and quicker salty vocabulary
(disguised in shallow semantics)
set the stage for
inevitable disaster.

Freaky leaders mingle
desperately seeking any
weak excuse to poorly perform
and, like a single straw,
they'll grab it.

Consumed by pomposity,
such blatant arrogance
is more
than merely,
some bad habit.

At this dark hour
real revelers are
fast asleep. Only a
cool breeze interrupts the
peace with raw rustling.

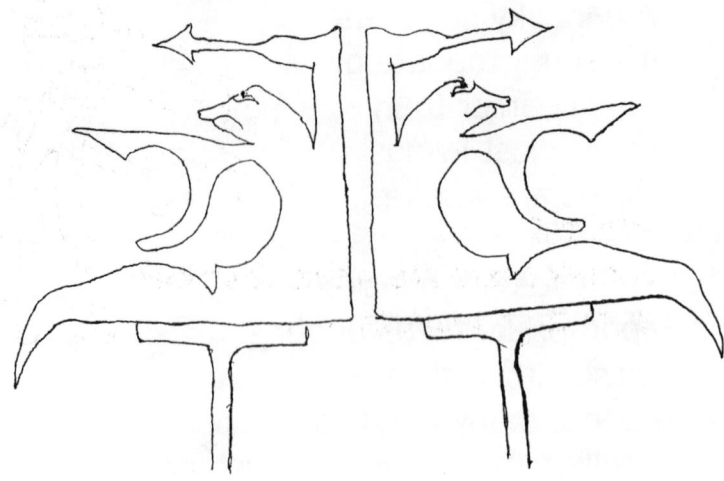

Can we afford this
crass movement toward extreme
political discord?

reasonable folks
do recoil at vicious
political turmoil.

There's something deadly
about political insurgency
when it's

undertaken mostly
with passionate, maniacal
urgency.

Political
cheerleaders are often described
as bottom feeders

Rocks & Politics

Ancient tiny beasts
Burrowed into rock;
Their shapes lie dormant
In dark time's distance.

It's no mystery that
Too often, the supposedly
Sublime existence of
A nation's political leader

Slips from History's pages,
Decays completely, leaving
Only buried reflections of
Another fossil-before-his-time.

Distinguish between
religion's political
disguise and true faith.

political power's
illusion is often
naughtily gaudy

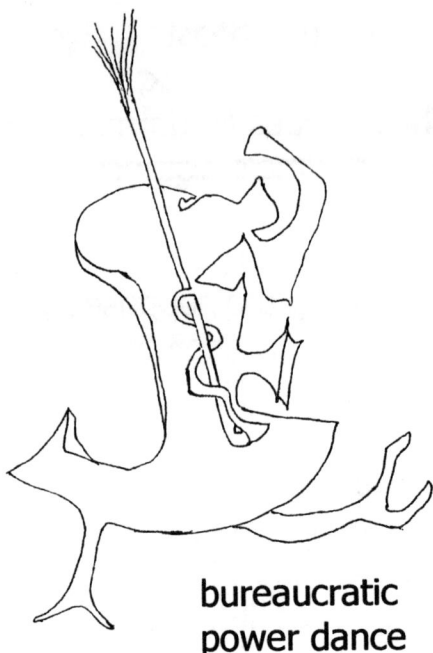

bureaucratic
power dance

All life loses its individuality
As a system develops to stomp
On our personal freedom.
A growing frustrated plurality

Has a tendency these days
To enjoy the trample.
No question the bitterness,
Anger, even viciousness of

This presidential pre-election
Debate has been quite ample.
What really scares me are the
Future elections of '08 and 2012.

Politics will have learned
Which human values should be
Spurned by past example.

Protecting us by Puritanically
Reducing our liberty suggests
We are committing social suicide.

It is an act unworthy of this Nation's
Character to falsely presume
Humanity can be legally purified

hypocrite no season
knows; political worms
turn as the wind blows.

Politicians should
Put their charm on a farm where
It can do less harm.

Each then goes and blows
His nose using issues as
Throw-away tissues.

Make this transition
Complete: prepare their own raw words
For them to eat.

If you must eat your
own words at least don't let them
get stuck in your throat

mistakes are often
made while minds listen to their
own quiet echoes.

Evils of contentious
Leaders: incompetence
And chicanery

A darker side of
Semantics could be politics'
Verbal antics.

Could politics quite
easily be defined as
the seat of deceit?

Only teaching one
what's incorrect's a form of
mental disrespect.

What a blessing to
discover some teachers have
the audacity

to inspire students
struggling to reach their
unique capacity.

100

An essence of
formal learning is to keep
students engaged – not caged.

BESIDE INTELLIGENCE

Most great teachers grab
students by the scruff of their
curiosity.

conflicting opinions
are caught in an attitude
rarely taught: to

consider controversial
thought as alternative
solutions sought.

beware noise from the
edu-bully boys; tolerate
particularly

their banging, clanging,
rattling reactionary
rituals

ACADEMIC OBESITY: The Either/Or Dilemma

A complete learning experience
should help to answer the question:
What is it we expect of ourselves?

Finally it is time to focus on our nation's educational virus which must be addressed as a crisis if we are to continue to survive as a creative human social order.

The No Child Left Behind mentality blends its poison into the wilderness of technologically inventive mind activity and one must be blind not to witness the suggestion of social decay thrust upon us. This all-encompassing, philosophically tempting attitude toward the learning-and-living-process has produced a generation of vicarious, mentally obese pseudo-homosapiens.

Façade has replaced Substance in our classroom, our entertainment, in scientific research and it even comes with interpersonal relationships.

Leadership in these areas of life hardly recognizes its own lack of integrity.

Particularly in learning experiences have we failed to blend a measure of right brain innovative/imaginative content into the left brain information-gathering system.

Accountability is identified within an intellectually active model but with narrow academic procedures. Will we continue to neglect collaborative learning? Will we ignore the broader impact of interdisciplinary adventures?

Stuffing our mental memorization centers without creative exercise produces predictable academic obesity.

This dilemma goes deeper than most educators are willing to admit. Either Art classes will be measured with traditional testing or dropped from the curriculum. Either Product (and *not* Process) is the primary curriculum focus or the art program is labeled spurious and ineffective. How shortsighted the conventional academic community has become!

The Either/Or pedagogic dictum has produced some of the most unfortunate, shortsighted programs in our public and private educational institutions.

Loaded with intellectual "fat", passion and personal focus are relegated to the cognitive closet's top shelf. Dressed in Hypocrisy's regalia, we are reassured that each student will be served as an individual within the system.

"Balderdash", I reply!

In Education's
joint, boring lectures have their
snoring counterpoint

Imagination provides
just enough madness
to free the mind
from Reality's handcuffs

Pitting reason against
disgrace is spitting with the
wind in your face.

104

intelligence sans
integrity and compassion
is black-hearted.

Testing to measure
intelligence is now an
anachronism

Learning custom's
facile form for accountability
needs reform.

Plans to develop
human growth continue on
a conventional

track – living with an
intellectual snack on
mind's short cul-de-sac

On wisdom's water
deceptive prophets sail aboard
ill-equipped craft.

Mind must balance
Freedom delicately with
Responsibility.

It's important to
distinguish between maintenance
and improvement.

106

critical decisions
should not affect life's breadth
but its depth; whereas,

influences of
broad breadth depend upon deep,
spiritual breaths.

Sometimes agile bodies
may house fragile minds and,
indeed, vice versa.

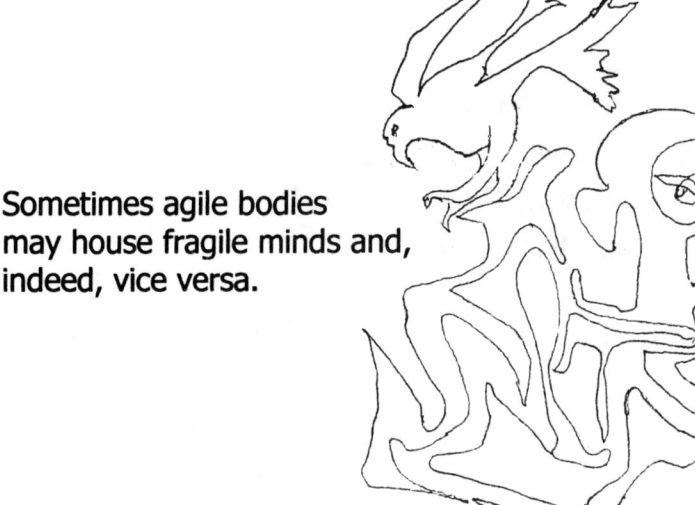

athletic competition
can yield collaboration
on the playing field;
but I regret

in our culture we've yet
to find a sharing experience
to bind the non-competitive
creative mind.

Tell me, where did we go wrong?
To what distinctive species do we belong?
Evolving like History's extinctive dinosaur's song,
We're dissolving temperamentally while physically strong.

Grading Procedure Follow-up

Several years after an article I wrote was published in Innovation Abstracts (Volume XXI, No. 3, Feb. 3, 1999) by NISOD at the University of Texas at Austin, Director Dr. Suanne D. Roueche permitted me to include it in book six, **Survival Weapons** on pages 48-53.

With minor changes, I have been using this grading system with my students as it was written in the essay, <u>Science and Soul of Learning Accountability</u>, for maybe close to 30 years. It occurs to me to follow up this process with some reactions from students who have experienced the fundamental visual arts program with me more recently. Student identifications have been omitted.

"This class was a very new experience for me. I have not taken an art course since 8th grade. I was exposed to many things I had never seen before, and found hidden talents I didn't dream I could possess. I came out with a much greater understanding and admiration for art. It was a pleasure to be in this class."

============

"I really liked your class. You made it fun and interesting. Unfortunately, I am a victim of procrastination. In all academic categories I procrastinate a lot. But I learned from your class how procrastination won't always get me by. I'm just sorry it had to be your class that made me realize it. I really wanted to show you my creative side. But due to my faults I could not. Overall, I loved your class though. You taught me important things I'll never forget and you've inspired me to draw more. Thanks to you, I will explore my creativity more and will be drawing a lot more pictures like I used to when I was younger. Thanks for everything, you're a great guy and I want to keep in touch."

============

"If I could do the course over, I would have liked to do a lot of the extra credit work. However, this time around I was always crunched for time and therefore didn't feel like I had the amount of time needed to do a good job. However, I really enjoyed the class and thought you assigned just enough work. I think your class is pretty great the way it is. Thanks for a great semester."

==========

"I enjoyed this class. Because I enjoy art and I liked the different style of teaching that you used. I got rather bogged down with my other studies and commitments in the second half of the semester. Although that's no excuse it does show why my performance was lacking a bit. Thank you for the doors you have opened in my mind."

=========

"I would have loved to show off the work that I could produce but it just didn't happen for me and it bothers me tremendously. I have a lot of absences and missed assignments. But I feel the grade I am requesting is fair because the work I did do I did with great effort, ability and enjoyment. I feel that I have learned or at least taken something away from this class – the most important – reintroducing myself to the art world and my artistic ability. Thanks Al for the talks and not giving me a hard time."

=========

NB: With each of the above five student comments was a request for a final grade I felt the student deserved. Developing academic integrity is an essential part of the learning process.

Creativity's
testosterone perpetuates
Fine Arts passion.

Future's unblemished
Truth: youth's curiosity
blended with concern.

Believe me: it isn't
So much *what* I make as it
Is *that* I make.

Men with more than dash
Develop courage, creativity
And cash.

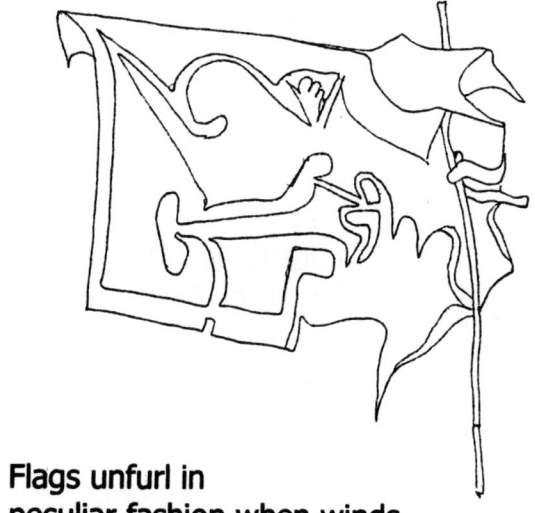

Flags unfurl in
peculiar fashion when winds
display extreme passion

when passion rejects
reason, the human race
alters its character.

Brevity has often
been perceived as third cousin
to Levity.

With sanctimonious
anger, confusion emerges;
guile surges.

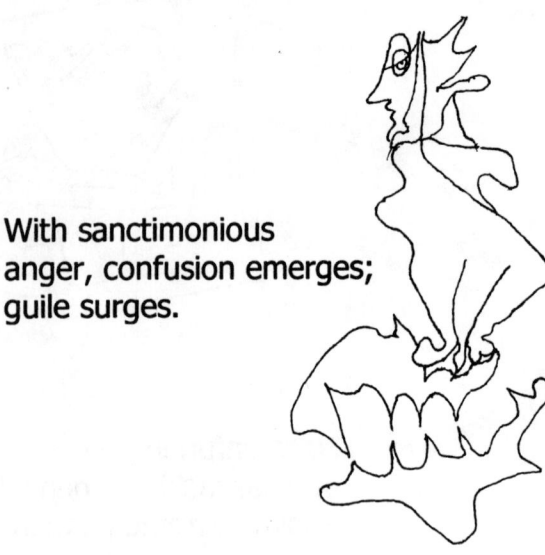

Some things will never
happen; don't get depressed.
Accept it and move on.

Disappointment's pose
reaches deeper than sour
surfaces disclose.

You say that I've got
Intermittent Explosive
Disorder? LIKE HELL!

Life seems driven by
choices one consistently
affords: seeds or swords

Uncertainty is
an unpleasant dish eaten
either raw or cooked.

Yes, even a bird
is prone to groan when one's mind
steps out on its own.

Curmudgeons are
anachronisms in a world
already screwed up.

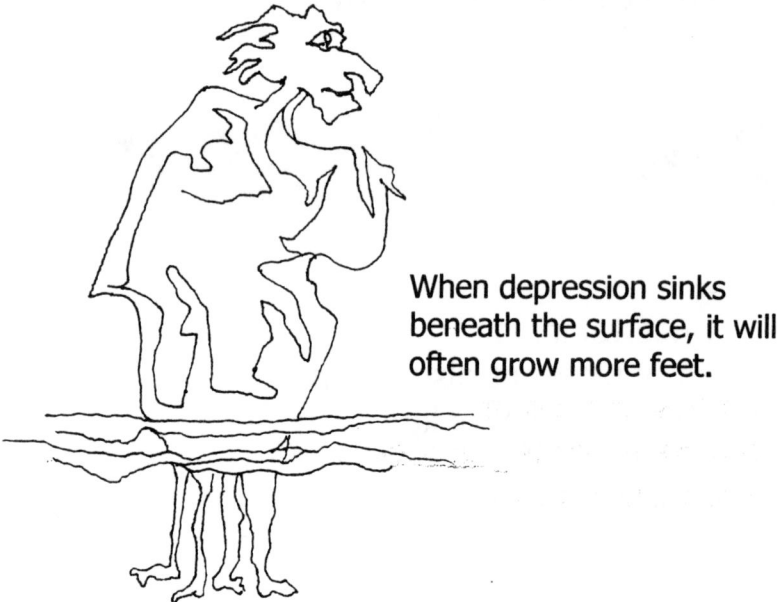

When depression sinks
beneath the surface, it will
often grow more feet.

When clothes you want to
wear don't fit, don't diet guys —
just rationalize.

It's not widely known:
Fate and Reality are
only stepsisters.

An assumption of
omnipotence is our species'
worst corruption.

With humans, Mind controls
Body; in politics,
Body controls minds.

Mental shards lay at
our leaders' feet: Compassion's
well out of fashion

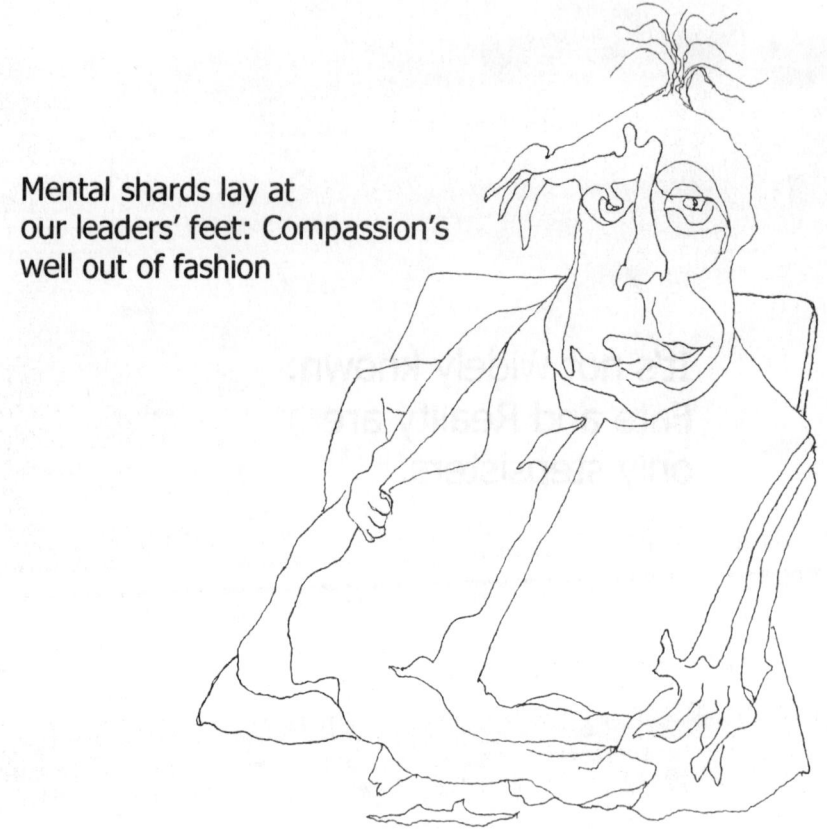

emotions overwhelm
reason: unbalanced
political season

IN THE END

with hearts pierced by
sorrow's arrow, tears flow from
emotion's bone marrow

when a close friend dies,
Death comes from its mental pocket
and bites the heart.

Some memories come
to bed with me; others are
shadows on the wall.

It is my privilege and pleasure to include in this book thoughts by journalist/educator Remy Benoit written to me during an internet conversation. And, with her permission, I share them with you:

"So often I feel like a child in a 'grown up land' where I don't know the rules, don't understand the underlying framework....

I listened in horror to that speech last night so filled with the duplicity of omission of the problems, the truths, of so very many, many things.

I don't understand why we constantly choose lies, avarice, bottom lines over truth, beauty, and love. All of life, all over the planet, ah, the entire universe, would be so much better if we chose the latter, as all the real needs of people for acceptance, for basic survival needs, for love, would be met. Imagine, just imagine, what the world would be like if we chose to bring out the best of everyone rather than their pain, their frustration, their angst?

What do they gain, those who stand for nothing real? lasting? soul filled? Are they so despairingly needy and vacuous that they just fill their own emptiness with fleeting "power over" rather than for real "power with?"

Maybe, perhaps, I am the one who is crazy...maybe I'm crazy because I believe the Creator meant us to live in wonder and awe at the beauty and the endless possibilities of the Creation; to share an ongoing Creation; somehow I just can't accept that we are here to "torture" out what we need of it, or out of each other.

Venting, I guess...Alice in Whateverland. Perhaps I really do need a keeper. Perhaps I always will be the child who, as long as she draws breath, will see the wonder of loving...and continue writing about it, and trying to live it, when it all seems such an impossible dream.

Remy Benoit - Author of Letty; Island Quilts; Peace, Now; and Loving. (http:/www.) welcomehomesoldier.com & niquahanam.com
    The Niquahanam Project: Help to Heal the World

Editorial: Struggle for Creative Compromise

Too often social manipulators dismiss
tradition merely as a large hungry lizard
relaxing in Progress's path.
History should not be equated
with Antiquity. Some might claim
that a few of our nation's leaders are
T-Rexes taking a bite out of Society's
future. Anomaly has no better friends
than these myopic playmates.

Lessons Learned and Innovative Thinking
are not necessarily contemporary enemies.
Logic is only one of several intelligent weapons
in the human closet. Inventive Thinking
throws a pretty good punch, too. Only a Cynic
refuses to store them on the same shelf.

Questions: Can Instinct poison progress?
Where does Intuition fit into Future's plans?

This I do believe: Today's passion for
Instant Gratification will become a scar
on Human Growth.

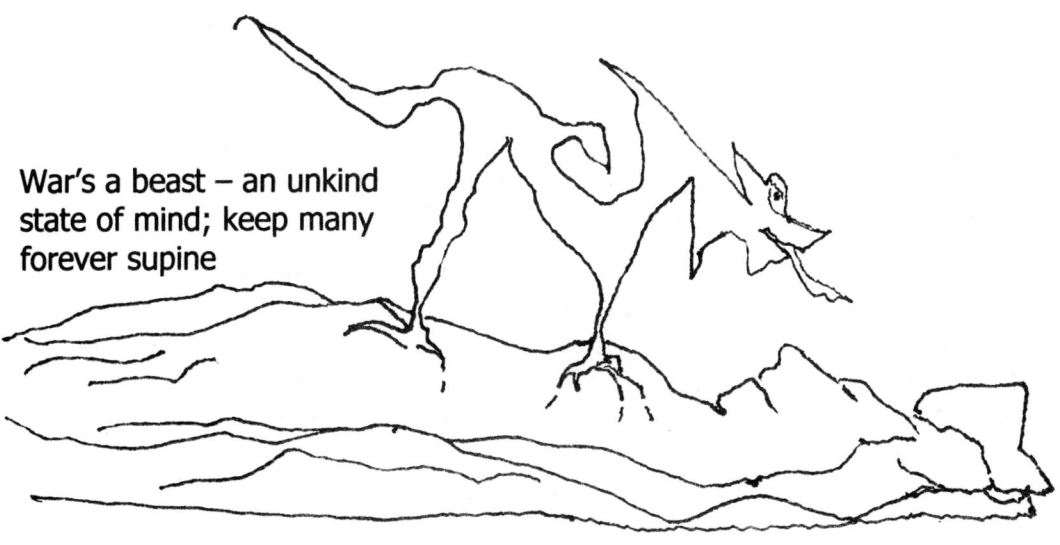

War's a beast – an unkind
state of mind; keep many
forever supine

Reality's chained
to coincidence, chance, or
even circumstance.

Too often, as
less-than-curious birds, we
only skim life's surface.

Finally, permit
me to add to my confusion:
while my mind

appears to move swiftly,
I've come to the conclusion
it's an illusion.

Urge this culture not to tolerate but encourage diversity.

BEYOND THE GRIPES – ABOVE THE SCARS

The reason I
love to laugh is because I'm
sadness intolerant.

When I get too
excited, something inside me
really wants to dance.

prepare to greet this
fact discrete: butterflies
only taste with their feet.

DREAMS OF NECTAR

Birthdays have
a special flavor –
one we're almost
certain to savor.

Whether it's in our
succulent youth or
that ancient time-worn
sixty-twoth.

Life must prepare for
one critical moment known
when a seed is sown.

regarding your 'thank you' note
a response to it
by way of "you're welcome"
emerges as less-than-chipper.

more to the point:
an embarrassed reply like
"Nooo...I thank YOU!"
would be appropriately hipper.

Reflections For Your Birthday

As children, few knew the forty years
of adventures one would face to
understand the slow pace it takes
to finally appreciate what personal
struggle, hope's wrestle with reality,
dedicated persistence and, of course,
delayed reward means.

Remember your first experience
climbing the playground's slippery
steps so you could enjoy the ride
down the slide? Some moments so
mild and others wild would fill your
childhood while you experienced both
the joyful shout as well as the sullen pout.

It took growing mental strength to
recognize instant gratification was only
a myth. And that the best Life can offer is
a treasure chest filled with compromises
and a good night's sleep. You, my lovely
daughter, are one of a very special breed
of human beings. I am so proud to know you.

Grandfatherhood
presents a handle on a child's
future just out of reach.

It has to do with
sharing one's past while
avoiding temptation to preach.

Blending a bizarre
connection with anxiety
to vicarious joy,

birthday gifts and
succulent snacks appear
to be a worthwhile ploy.

Imagination
provides every life
a sliver of hope,

simultaneously
preserving Fundamentals
tied together with DNA's rope.

And while these two
generations are focused
on their own special needs,

both possess
universal empathy
on which humanity feeds.

Good friends now gone
are still with us. Not in body but
human nature's cruising spirit.

Choosing a special moment
of past connection: celebrate,
then prepare to endear it.

John Brigham

Power of a good life
reaches beyond one's
words to address it.

No one more deserves
our praise; nevertheless it
stirs in each of us who

remember John Brigham
as a man of moral strength
and passion to express it.

How will we live content
to understand the extent of
human nature's need to profess it

without our companion who
shared with us his vital spirit and
whom we must celebrate as blessed?

Bless you, John. You were
an inspiration we were so
very fortunate to touch.

Philosopher, counselor, friend
and poet. For all of us who know it,
we thank you – thank you so much.

Consider soul's three
Windows: Genetic, Aesthetic,
Empathetic.

emptiness may be
rewarding only when one
is prepared for it.

Epiphany transcends
formal, conventional
learning processes.

Sing a song of years gone by
And what rationale may we apply
for which we all can sanctify
this unexpected lullaby.

Age is a page Time's wrought
with occasional thought
which might outrage any
suitably sensitive sage.

And as it wears, at least
one fragile edge tears;
Protected only by our
pledge of prudent prayers.

I haven't heard a single word
from some good long-ago friends.
Where are they now? Someone tell
me how to get in touch again?

(Whatchya beendoin?
An-whereya been?
I'll bet yagot something brewin
((grin-grin-grin)). Help me quit my
curious stewin before it becomes
my unctuous undoin.

Holiday Poem '04

Such celebrations as Christmas,
Hanukkah, Kwanza or Ramadan
offer instinctive soul-nurturing
experiences more fulfilling than
associated gifts, special songs,
tradition's drinks, symbols or
history-kissed hypotheses.

Humanity must occasionally
reach into its mental mist,
beyond romance, ritual and
religious tryst to touch with
poetic fingertips that part of
passion which ignites a fire's
appetite whose flame acts as

spiritual suture: kneading our
past while feeding our future.
We enter this sacred space with
profound thoughts' sound --
greeting a gracious treasure
greater than one can measure
in sky, sea or holy ground.

Holidays are spent inadequately
with expressions of blatant joy
or latent love; but, perhaps,
caught briefly bent in the dear
sudden flight of a mourning dove.
It would be tragic if we could
express quite clear what it was.

Passion would then lose its magic.
Now how might one know it
if no one can show it? Answer:
Go make your intention to
uncover this wonder of another
dimension with imagination's
festive invention.

On Competition's
list I'm best known as a
Varsity Hedonist.

We read so much
About sunshine's touch.

If one truly understood why
Long distances may mystify,
While nigh-gentle light of a firefly
Urges fascination for it, and, as such,
Inspires us with a nearby optical sigh;

These beautiful moments are not harsh –
They're shy.

With very hot tea
it helps to initially
sip it with eyes closed.

Valentine Thinking

Here before us is a brief pause
In a myopic calendar of ego-applause
To celebrate a special aspect of human health.

It suggests limits for our praise of
Self extension and raise a blazon,
Brazen fourth dimension to reach beyond

One's personal shelf and accept the opportunity
To investigate treasured empathy measured
As an undeniable form of potential wealth.

Why it falls like a mental splinter
Within a vicious month of winter
Continues to annoy and befuddle.

And using a cliché heart shape as reason
To promote flowers out of season (as well as
Candy for the fat?) now that's not too subtle.

Move Valentine's Day to September and maybe
We'll remember Love's finest, most precious hour
As metaphorical flame colors the autumn's bower.

With two top lumps and a lower point
This world has constructed the logo-shrine
For a love-joint we continue to call valentine.

All should lament the distortion of our
Indispensable human anatomical design.
Let's alter the cliché symbol and develop a

Metaphor much more benign. Vertically slice
The simple "heart" in two. Now lay the shape
Horizontally on the floor (one half of it will do).

Note how it resembles a door-jamb (damn!)
How ideal that this heart part can properly
Function and prepare us for romance, - see?

When providing a permanently open
Mental door which will keep us
Receptive to fresh, flexible fancy.

Valentine Thoughts '05

Distinguished narration appears erratic
Beginning with a third century traumatic
Death of a blessed saint
Which later evolved into romantic celebrations
With candy and ribbons and the brightest red paint.

Nothing it seems could be more emblematic
Unless it might be a bouquet aromatic.
But blend Roman mystery with religious tradition
And produce Love Goddess's Cupid –
His history as a sweet winged magician

Who encouraged both the shy and fruitfully phlegmatic
To share this celebration in a melodramatic
(If still somewhat commercial) expression of feeling
With a now familiar heart-shaped symbol
That's forever appealing.

Many claim sharing this gift is symptomatic
Of one's love and devotion (although in truth problematic).
So send out your Valentines after careful selection
And guaranteed you'll be expressing
A personal form of authentic affection.

EPILOGUE

There is no question that my writing has been deeply affected by the near half-century in which I have been an educator/artist. I feel a sense of humility whenever I reflect on my diverse abilities.

It has been an honor to live a life in which my creative thinking has made a difference to so many others.

Frankly, it is a validation that affective learning is as critical to developing the whole person as is the conventional definition of intellect.

It has been my privilege to have been on the Educators' Endangered Species List for nearly fifty years (over three decades associated with Culver-Stockton College). Although I have often been identified as Culver-Stockton's resident Coyote, this has not been my home.

For each of us, no matter what age or circumstance, we have no home but the spaces in our mind. How comfortable we are within those spaces; what we fill them with; whether we keep up and clean them occasionally, these are the critical questions we carry with us for a lifetime.

Despite the fact I did travel throughout the world numerous times, I have been, over the years, overwhelmed more by the things I've *never* seen but continue to believe in. My imagination and creativity are a substantial part of the furniture in the space I call home. It is the faith in this space which keeps me going. There is a very impressive resource which says: "Faith is the substance of things not seen." Just as importantly, I have been continually impressed by four pieces of advice I received from several people I continue to admire. For what these are worth, I pass them along to you:

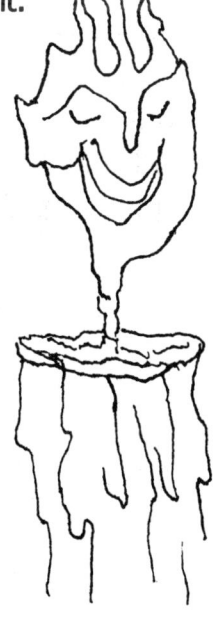

1. Do what you have to do before you have to do it.
2. Never give up.
3. Never slow down.
4. Never grow old.

137

ABOUT THE AUTHOR

I keep speculating on why I have been so vibrant in my later years of life. Sustaining creative energy seems to be an aspect of my focus. Of course I want to make these final years as fulfilling as possible. Only two of my elderly heroes are Georgia O'Keeffe and Frank Lloyd Wright. Each kept their brain exercising into their 90s. And although my memory keeps putting details onto a mental back burner, much of my intuitive nature has flourished by taking up new residence with visual and verbal passions.

As a youth, I worried a great deal about being different and yearned to be a part of the group socially. Now I revel in my individuality. Whether I'm playing my banjo and singing a folk song I have written, shaping a new clay vessel, germinating the seeds of my heirloom veggies for their spring planting, intuitively drawing a new beast-metaphor, writing a haiku, psy-ku, philoso-ku or even longer poem, inventing a collaborative imaginative game for young or old, this is an exciting time of life.

138

Sad memories make
a heart wrinkle. Joyful ones
give it a twinkle.

ABOUT THE AUTHOR – ANOTHER PERSPECTIVE

The people who make the best leaders are those who have once been lost themselves. When Al Beck, Professor of Art at Culver-Stockton for thirty years, attended college in the 1950s, he loved almost everything about it.

"I was not that focused on academia. I just wanted to have fun," said Beck. "I wanted to stay there. I just didn't like classes."

His father's job was to make sure that all the people coming to the United States from Europe after World War II could find jobs throughout the United States. Now if he could only find a job for his son.

Beck first entered the School of Drama at Northwestern University. "I had real problems memorizing lines," he said.

His next major was physical education.

While working on making whistles for class, a football player came up to him and needed help. "I'm saying to myself, 'What the hell am I doing in college making a whistle for a football player? Is this really what I want to do with my life?'"

His uncle, a famous psychologist on the faculty, got him in the School of Psychology where Beck promptly failed the first course.

A buddy then told him to take an art course. All you have to do is show up, try drawing and you get a C. "I said, 'Are you kidding? That's the greatest thing I've ever heard,' " Beck said. "I needed a C in order to stay in school so my old man wouldn't kick me out."

In his first class, everybody had to turn in three drawings a week.

"The teacher looks at my three drawings and says, "Al, you draw real good.' I looked at him and mumbled, 'Bullshit'." Beck said, "I came back the next week and I had 93 pages of drawings in the book completed."

His career has taken him from 10 years as a high school art teacher to Dean of Students at the Kansas City Art Institute to Culver Stockton in 1968. At Culver, he taught drawing, painting, ink work, printmaking, pottery and photography.

Though an art educator, Beck's philosophy applies to us all. "There are two things you want in your life. You want to have fun, and you want to work hard," Beck said. "Those of you that work hard but don't have fun, you're in trouble. Those of you that are having fun, and you're not working hard, you're in even more trouble. It's that combination that makes a life worthwhile."

Bill Schlegl, Journalist – Quincy Herald Whig, Quincy, IL.

Books In Print

Other wondrous works by AL Beck

GNOMES & POEMS $10.00

AL's first book, a collection of almost absurd drawings and completely cured poetry. "AL Beck is witty, playful, and having fun with words ... reminding me of a giddy Ogden Nash."
* Dr. Sam Grabarski

140

Analysis does have
its aberration.
I've been cynical
about some pedagogues'
clinical appreciation
of my efforts.
There are claws
in their applause.

SIGHT LINES $6.00

Poems and drawings, which "are delight-ful - full of life with no strained metaphors! We found ourselves laughing aloud and reading poems to each other."
* Nola Ruth

Tele-transmission dysfunction

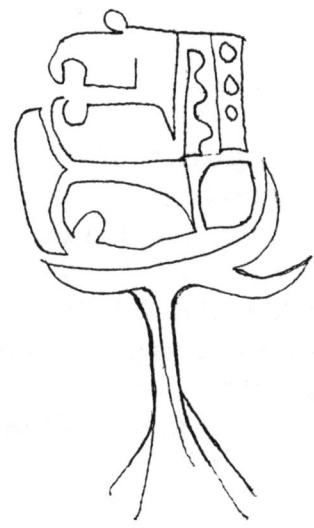

SONGS from the RAINBOW WORM $9.50

Poems, drawings, photographs and ceremonial masks. "AL Beck's book features a number of poems and illustrations that truly reflect the author's wisdom and awareness."
  * Lee Shunji Nishida

BEAUCOUP HAIKU $10.00

Haiku poetry and drawings. "AL Beck captures life from the side-door that most have thought was closed for good. Part Woodstock, part Pete Seeger and part Gary Larson, he weaves his pen at a level that is just a bubble or two from plumb."
  * John Tripp

GOD IS IN THE GLOVE COMPARTMENT
$10.00

Haiku poetry and drawings. "Think of AL Beck as the Good-Humor man. Be it poem or art, he will get to you, and enrich your outlook on life."
** * David A Wilson**
"Beck's poetry marries imagination and wisdom."
** * Deb Rosenberg**

SURVIVAL WEAPONS $10.00

142

Poetry, drawings and *autobiographitti*. "I'm having a great time, immersed in your poetry. I've read the books cover to cover and am having another go at it. From being aroused to rolling over in laughter to interesting grand thought, I'm enjoying thoroughly."
** * Phyllis Dopp**

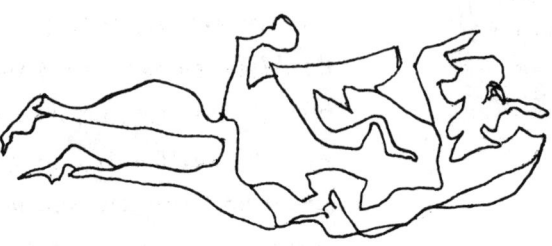

a Neo-con irrelevantly wrapped

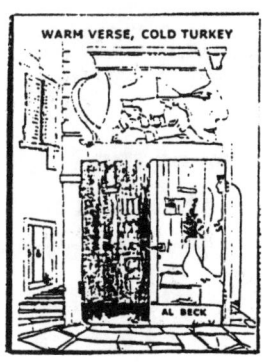

WARM VERSE, COLD TURKEY $10.00

"Fantastic! You are a major part of the mystical construct surrounding the learning process. You are the magician! ... you are the sage ... You know the way through the maze and you tell them how to use 'the force' to get there. They will get their strength and courage by connecting to the words of the sage."
  * James Burns

Frosty morning's first
light – quiet woods; even the
angels are sleeping.

143

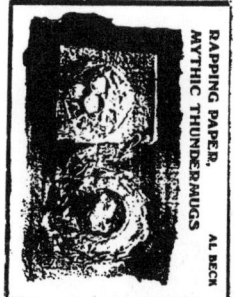

RAPPING PAPER, MYTHIC THUNDERMUGS
$10.00

Yo! Big Daddy does it again – tickling our tummies with his wit. His haiku delves the depths of understanding while at the same time lightening our lives with humor's different outlook. With AL's contributions, civilization as we know it comes to an end! putting us ahead in the game.
  * David A Wilson

CONVERSATIONS WITH LIZARD'S BONES AND WIZARD'S STONES $12.00

"AL Beck gives a great overview of the highs and lows of teaching and the institution of education with all its flaws and how to overcome them. There are profound thoughts simply told for those new and old to education. The poems, stories, songs and illustrations LEAP out at you ..."
    * Marjan Glavac

LIFEPSYCHLES $14.00

AL is an artist in all definitions of the word: visual, literary and performing, showing great passion for all of the arts. Beck takes you deep inside a very personal side of his mind ... amazingly revealing of his innermost spiritual being. AL Beck is truly a modern day renaissance man.
    * Kristi Cornett

144

postpaid from: AL Beck
                5987 County Road 231
                Monroe City, MO 63456